Mothersong

Also by Amy Acre

Pamphlets
And They Are Covered in Gold Light
Where We're Going, We Don't Need Roads

As editor
Field Notes on Survival
Alter Egos
The Dizziness of Freedom

Mothersong

AMY
ACRE

BLOOMSBURY POETRY

LONDON · OXFORD · NEW YORK · NEW DELHI · SYDNEY

BLOOSMBURY POETRY
Bloomsbury Publishing Plc
50 Bedford Square, London, WC1B 3DP, UK
29 Earlsfort Terrace, Dublin 2, Ireland

BLOOMSBURY, BLOOMSBURY POETRY and the Diana logo
are trademarks of Bloomsbury Publishing Plc

First published in Great Britain, 2023

Hip, Hip, Hoorah! © Karel Appel Foundation / DACS 2023

A catalogue record for this book is available from the British Library

ISBN: PB: 978-1-5266-5069-6; eBook: 978-1-5266-5068-9;
ePDF: 978-1-5266-5067-2

2 4 6 8 10 9 7 5 3 1

Typeset by Laura Jones
Printed and bound in Great Britain by
CPI Group (UK) Ltd, Croydon CR0 4YY

To find out more about our authors and books
visit www.bloomsbury.com and sign up for our newsletters

For Billie, the brave

IN THE WET-AIRED TRENCHES
OF THE TUBE I WAS

a tigress, cub in jaw, sniffing out cordite
and saltpetre, spying warshapes in the dark.
I saw the parched black mouth of the track,
a long, marauding animal, limbless slither,
crabapple on tongue. My child, months
from the womb, hung from my teeth.
I ferried her by the neck and saw her death
everywhere. I hung on the grit-kissed wall
until the train pummelled in to replace
imagination. Forgive me, I saw things
I couldn't tell my therapist. I mauled
thought to silence and counted my steps
and talked to myself in dissertation. I saw
others, smelt their milk in the slow lifts,
smiled at their litters and wondered if
they too saw their babies fall, if they fought
escalators tumbling with fear, if we were
all staring down the same muzzle, waiting
for the grip to drop from our own hands.

T-MINUS FORTY WEEKS

two people in love break apart in reverse

      break, return   a fizz flute smashed into crazing

holds its glass curve   fist plums into palm   a lick

of fresh chromosome   sinks in your throat

      dying backwards   we are unkissed, busy   under

        our lamp of hall light   groan against loving

      split at the apex   spill

    into river, knowing

    this is how we make room

      our fingers leave

      prints

        the bed

      dips   in the

      middle the

          v

      in   love

BILLIE, BLINDED BY GRACE

She wakes at six: bonsai in a wood
of straight pines, *book* between her teeth.
There is a witch, a ginger plait, dog,
bird, frog, dragon. Night still in my bones, I
beg gravity for patience but my kneecaps
are obtuse angles collapsing. We fall
into morning. Two slices. No sugar.
Glastonbury on iPlayer. Our sweat
unscented by portaloos, firepit smoke, knock-
off highs or the hope of a nameless mouth.
Two hundred thousand warm skulls.
Webs of gland. And Stormzy, building
a church. Orange joggers, choir, confetti.
Our sofa a pew hard as shellac. Now
it is more comfortable to stand. Now it is
more comfortable to reach as if a better me
lived in the ceiling, to bend, head low,
arse high, hair the rolling wave of a thousand
lighters but this isn't lighters waving. It's
skyrockets, bass, ballet and fuck Boris. And if
we could. And come. And here, and here
I am unwound, footwork and wilding.
Little tree, cross-rooted, follows my feet,
sway of lash. I sweep and we are up, down,
spinning. Sometimes I go so long
without music inside me, I forget there is
living in its wavy lines, that blood needs
cadence, this living left in all the spaces
before I became. Dive bars and dance halls,

dirty raves, Year 10 dry ice and parquet. Hips
quicker than Clint. How the podiums
found me. How I would teach a room
to move, body lapping a mind that ran
behind, burning blister and love.

DADDY PIG

Once a time. This Daddy. This Mummy.
This babies. Whee-oh! Whee-oh! Whee-oh!
Uh oh. Don't worry. The end.
—Billie

at two this kid knows jeopardy
that without it we have no story

that without story we are no one
that no one is just someone who wasn't saved

someone was saved is the story:
the pups save the monkeynaut

daddy pig drops his keys down the drain
and mr bull digs up the road

milk soothes a gumsore smile
as new teeth pull up a chair

at two she knows jeopardy but not how
it shifts when you're done growing

how danger's a growing stack of envelopes
how your phone is the face of a predator

and a predator is your own face
in photographs glancing offstage

5

in terror and confusion
pig eyes digging up the road

it is terrible and confusing
to be the same story day after day

to look over the edge but never smash
you see a piece of yourself on the ground

and just leave it there
maybe you'll come back to it later

ATHEISM

dear lord, fix my broken vagina that I may climb the tree of longing and find myself in its branches, feet tucked under knees, pleated skirt and no pants. let the freckles on my husband's arm tickle not my heart but lower, let the music of my cunt sing like the hot tap or the vibrato of the throat attached to rash hands dripping with their own enemy. dear lord, make porn better, or good porn cheaper, or just make me richer. let the blonde on the tube platform bend again to tie her shoes when I'm alone. let my husband clean the bath or fix a fault in the pipes that I may find him on his knees, earth-greased arms holding the house up, behind him a perfect pout. dear lord, let our daughter not wake as I guide his face to my waistband. dear lord, please fix my broken vagina because I have so many tasks in the day and I need something. I have already changed the sheets. dear lord, I am tired of thinking about nuns or schoolgirls or rape, I want to live in his eyes, I want my body to strike, to strobe on the bed with us and not slink, a smudge on the wallpaper or draft tweet. I am scared that I've politicised touch to the point where I have cancelled my own desire and I am tired, I am so fucking tired all the time. dear lord, I used to have an awesome vagina. it got everything right and made friends easily. dear lord, since leaving home I have belonged to twenty-one houses. if you leave skin everywhere I must be paper. dear lord, it's me at fourteen, held by hands I recall more clearly now there is a smaller me running through the house. dear lord, when he holds me close I am butter from the fridge, sticking to rip and impossibly stiff but I remember what it feels like to melt, I know I am in here somewhere

Let's say it's nineteen-eighty. Let's say it's a Friday.
My sister is turning five. In Norway,
a drilling rig lies belly up in the North Sea.
In Washington, a rock blows smoke rings.
Everywhere, people are in love with Debbie Harry.
My sister, thinned with flu, pale smiles beside a Smarties cake.
Evening undoes its dresscoat, lengthens on the sofa.
A fat palm slaps the headtop of a fuzzing box
and it comes into picture: a woman and man are in love
in the shadow of a courthouse,
in the phoenix of a family.
On cotton begonia spread, her Rossetti hair corrugates
like a pull-down ladder. His voice is the colour
of a blood orange and they are in love.
They are loving, as zeros uncurl on solicitor bills,
as brothers and sisters design midnight feasts.
Between them, a dream of the present sleeping
sweetly inside a future where love resembles itself.
When they have risen wild as ghosts, given all,
the man grips her legs in his hands, lifts them
into a capsized letter A. Gravity blows them a kiss
and somewhere in the penstrokes of life, I begin. Small gallop.
Two weeks later, Sartre dies lung-first in Paris
and in London, a county court smiles.
At three weeks, after a bloodless concert, the woman
takes rain to a chemist. When she exits,
all she can hear is Bach's *Brandenburg No. 3*,
my hooves where pain should be.

THE RABBI'S DAUGHTER

the rabbi's daughter
let me try on
her swimsuit while
our parents drank
in the garden

led me to
the bathroom
said the suit
was *waterproof*
you could wee
straight through
so i did and
she watched

before we ran
to the depths
of the blow-up pool
and when i think
of this i think
of her father
leading me

through a door
him asking how
it would feel
on the bimah
no father to applaud

of saying *empty*
my careful picking
the performance
more exact than
my big day

noting the smudge

when as sometimes
happens we are called
upon to give away
our stream to make
fine music of our pain

AZRAEL

at the age you are now your father's body
had built a nest for an angel

you   key stage two   couldn't place why
he coughed wingbeats   cried shameless

the year white coats saw the stowaway
photobomber in a radio wave

today   tapping forty   your neck convexes
you bookmark testaments

nothing makes sense like a toddler walking around
with your face hurling a sippy cup at the wall

this summer we're home braising our skirting boards
and the bees are brave

buzzing thickets comfort crushed shale into shade
and you run to remember not all angels are hereditary

in one version god drops a leaf
and seven billion eyes read your name

forty days later a test card

this summer we cling to our tvs like gastropods on a rock
the land before time washes up on netflix

11

littlefoot's mum is dead like simba's dad is dead like
bambi's mum is dead like bastian's mum is dead

if this is how we level up to protagonist
you'd rather swim in the shadow of a demiurge

you swing your daughter dizzy in the garden
to remember not all childhoods are hereditary

at the age you first met memory
she spies her shadow   takes it everywhere

but watches mama dinosaur die dry eyed
while you break on the black friday couch

four thousand wings trying you on for size
wonder why your kid's hypothetical loss stings

sharper than your lived one
you ask your mother

she says when the angel came she couldn't look
directly at your grief   a wooden doll inside hers

you say kids are resilient   you were ok   she says
you weren't though   were you

THE YEAR OF THE HORSE

After Giles Goodland

Twentysomethings geeked out over the World Wide Web
while polyamorous malware circled in hoodies.

Thatcher toppled like a graven image and I wrote a school news
report on her fall, gleefully dictated by my mum.

Green-collar workers looked for a connection between hand gel
and transmissible spongiform encephalopathies.

I met a large grey bear in a South London hospital. Microplastic
props accumulated in McMansions. Dad died.

The crime wave was high with muggings mysterious. Earth
waited for a shout-out from air formerly known as wall.

I would have given anything for a stick blender, or a soundbar,
or a black hat, or a lithium-ion battery.

SEE ALSO

Dad is a see also of **mum**. **Mum** is a see also of **dad**.

As nouns the difference between **mum** and **dad** is that **mum** is (chiefly|UK|informal) **mother** or **mum** can be a chrysanthemum or **mum** can be silence or **mum** can be a sort of strong beer, originally made in Brunswick, Germany while **dad** is (informal) a **father**, a male parent.

As an adjective **mum** is (colloquial) silent.
As an interjection **mum** is stop speaking! hush!
As a verb **mum** is to act in a pantomime or dumb show.

As proper nouns the difference between **Mum** and **Mother** is that **Mum** is one's **mother** while **Mother** is one's **mother**.

As a noun **mother** is one (human) who (a) has (raises) a child (b) gives birth (c) donates a fertilised egg or (d) donates a body cell resulting in a clone or **mother** can be something that is the greatest or most significant of its kind or **mother** can be (euphemistic|coarse|slang) motherfucker or **mother** can be (nonstandard) a cat that catches moths.

As a noun **father** is one (human) who (a) has (raises) a child (b) provides sperm or (c) donates a body cell resulting in a clone.

As verbs the difference between **mother** and **father** is that **mother** is to perform mothering; to nurture while **father** is to be a **father** to; to sire.

As nouns the difference between **mummy** and **daddy** is that **mummy** is an embalmed corpse wrapped in linen bandages for burial, especially as practised by the Ancient Egyptians while **daddy** is (LGBTQ|slang) (a) an (typically) older man sexually involved with a younger male or (b) a (typically) butch or masculine-presenting lesbian in a dominant role or acting as teacher, guide or breadwinner in a sexual relationship.

As a noun **mama** is (hypocoristic|usually|childish) **mother**, female parent or **mama** can be a sexually attractive, mature woman while **Big Mama** is an owl character voiced by Pearl Bailey in Disney's 1981 feature film *The Fox and the Hound* and **yo mama** is a reference to a person's **mother** frequently used to insult the target preying on widespread sentiments of filial piety and typically combined with suggestions of promiscuity, unattractiveness, obesity, laziness, poverty, stupidity or poor hygiene.

As a title **mother superior** is a prioress or nun in charge of a religious order or house of women under vows or **mother superior** can be a song by Good Riddance, Katzenjammer or Coheed and Cambria.

As a title **father** is a priest or religious leader authorised to perform the sacred rituals of a religion, especially as a mediatory agent between humans and one or more deities or **father** can be God as in the first person of the Holy Trinity.

As direct (adult) forms of address the difference between **mummy** and **ma** is that **mummy** drives an Audi or other marque of luxury vehicle headquartered in Ingolstadt, Bavaria as a subsidiary of parent company, the Volkswagen Group.

As play or make-believe **mummy** is a toy or bear and co-carer of a smaller toy or baby bear. **Mummy** sleeps in the bed with baby bear and big baby but (sometimes) **mummy** is lost or (sometimes) **mummy** is stuck behind the dryer or the couch or falls through a grate or **mummy** can be a catcher for milk or urine or **mummy** can be a bad guy or naughty mummy.

As an adjective **mummy** is mum-like or matronly.
As an adjective **mummy** is undesirable or post-prime and poorly dressed except where **mummy** is yummy in which case the opposite is true.

As a noun a **motherboard** is the main printed circuit board (PCB) in general-purpose computers and other expandable systems, often referred to as the **mother** of all components attached to it, which often include peripherals, interface cards, and daughterboards or **motherboard** can be a deep-sea octopus, known as *Graneledone boreopacifica* and observed in the Monterey Submarine Canyon.

The difference between **mothership** and **motherland** is that **mothership** is a bat signal or calling, no less than twenty per cent light while **motherland** is an arable quilt, including any of a number of types of dense bread, brack or bun often containing dried fruits.

BIOLUMINESCENCE

If you are alive, you produce some light.
—Ann Makosinski

brush of bear   neon sunrise   screed

  of upstart filaments   gestalt pelt

        soft bulb of you

lightbox atop shoulders

        brush of bear   I scroll fibres into

flipbook

        filter you in crema   juno

love   glowworm spell   brush of bear

  homogenic tresses   each

  a falling tree   dark winter sky

X X

For J

i boy for you
sly clit anthurium
cutting-edge tits
spangled off
as sports bra
freedom a foothold
inside a new body
inside another
reach into tilled earth's
tangled roots
pull out my cock
music stiffening
against you
sometimes
i need to shock
your body
into iambs
hold your hips
in the blind light
of a bad street
flower gut
muscle and fist
find your unnamed
towns in the sistine
light of early

ORIGIN STORY

you with your smell of yeast, of self-raising flour, of four-day
pyjamas, of fingernail gunge, of red wire forest, of splinters, of
gum disease, of mountain lion, of papa bear, of shitty finger, of
crackle, of clean sweat, of whiskey and raisins, of old coppers, of
wet holey soles, of scottish sunrise, of tumble, of terrors, of
alcohol sweetening, of umami kale, of durum, of ink, of puzzle paper, of sheet rivers, of dirty sunshine, of plaid of colours of marvel,
of soggy elastic, of morning tongue, of adenoid, of spit and slam,
of city eviction, of grassy lullabies, of berries and smoke,
of six men in a kitchen, of a hundred and ten covers, of wall moss,
of lost pavement, of gyratory flyover, of white concrete, of brown
blood, of splatter, of congealed, of warm, of oil, of puddles, of
tree trunks, of potato dust, of promise, of strap, of snap, of
pomelo wax, of ironic daisies, of colourless jelly, of spread-eagle
larynx, of one more, of undrunk tea, of slanted toast, of sly cheek,
of spider scratch, of cheese stretch, of syrup, of die for, of wood, of
would, of lark's head, of jute, of wrap, of span, of spoon, of oceany
iris wet storm of my hunger, of this, of rock and paper, of one
more, for you, for you, I would

DANCE ON MY GRAVE

In St Mary's Garden,
Billie is jumping on graves.
I try to catch her, unruly
pigeon, winging between
broken sundial, benches
that remember. She wants
me to dance with her
among the dogs and tilia,
stone chests and hart's-
tongue and I try to explain,
someone's under there.

Dance on My Grave was
a book I stole from school.
Library plastic-wrapped
thrill about two boys:
Southend geeks who held
each other from the ground
up. One, uprooted,
kept holding, while
the other became earth,
swallowing still
in the flower of grief

and as I read, I plunged
my tips into dirt, downing
fistfuls of queer and
glowing language,
rose and petalled,

my Cyberdog-dyed head
a many-coloured
baptisia spread, inhaled,
and concealed between
pages. Time capsule
to raise later.

A character actor
I can't place pretends
not to see us. I keep my eyes
on the slabs. Billie
kicks in tap, tails and top
hat holding a leaf, knows,
without knowing,
how rationed sunlight
– death's withholding –
makes us want
to turn up the bass.

There's nothing quiet
about the dead. Nitrogen
ghosts fibrillate soil into
spring that births birdsong.
Coral bells are bursting,
budding or spent and
I think of pissing in bushes,
the way bark feels
against your bare back,
dark yards haunted
by lighters and cider.

Child of mine sways,
resurrects a chorus
line of vertebrae.
I cave, rest on the
unwritten corner
of a ledger stone,
I'm sure they won't mind,
and keen for the thunder
if I were to rise in rhythm,
lift a boot and slam
it down, feel the dirt
give me back.

ELECTRICITY: A BUYER'S GUIDE

If you want to know I'll tell you
about having an affair
with your own husband,

electrons stored and spoiling,
the unkissed curve of thigh on him
as he carries her to a tiny bed.

About crashing through idiots
at Old Street with third-date fever,
thinking only of home and her

small face broadening, elephant
dance to my knees. Between us,
we chase the nine invisible

points of a circle, lights flicking
off and on in the circuit board
of our home where the neighbours

rain flowers on each other
all night, throat-ache red
and flashing blue, but always

a smile for our sunshine. There is
a rainbow on our window,
there is a shadow over our bed.

We prop our couch cushions
to the downstairs glass,
meet in borrowed light

while evening preheats
across the marsh, my face in his neck
like it's the last time.

ICE BABY

When I hear what is happening in America I turn back on myself,
crouch on the landing where no light falls and wait for the piglet
in her sniffle to unlung. Like I know the full farmyard of her
discontents and which corn snack to invoke against rainfall, I know
no bailiff is coming to box me in a van, god-complex me from her.
No vested blizzard will surprise me on the dawn shift when I'm
slow-eyed and puttyesque. No fat-fisted plucker will pick her from
school for a fresh-painted purgatory to watch other kids crack,
gnawing on chalk ends as twilight comes knocking, keeping her cry
for my step. I will not exchange my biography for the role of deterrent.
Her face will grace neither Twitter storm nor petition. She will not
be raised by ghosts and forget the arrangement of my voice.
Her fire will not be quashed under a bleeding flag but over there
they are freezing and the president is so afraid. Over there the children
are freezing, the mothers are freezing, the fathers are freezing,
the supply teachers, the accountants and Uber drivers and poets,
the potwashes and lawyers are freezing, the orphans and stepkids.
Their gloves have gone fuzzy, they are layering their tights and blowing
into each other's faces. They are drinking white spirit and weeping
into photographs. They are avalanche and they are the climbers
twitching under vast white rock and I look only long enough to
turn up her covers and remember this has nothing to do with us.

MARGARET GARNER WILL HAVE HER REVENGE ON KENTUCKY

Found text from the *Cincinnati Gazette*, January 29, 1856

arrest of **fugitive** slaves
a slave **mother** murders her child
rather than see it **returned** to slavery
great excitement existed throughout **the** city
the whole of yesterday, in **consequence of** the arrest of **a party of** slaves, and the **murder** of **her child**
by a slave mother while the officers were in the act
of making the arrest. a party of seventeen slaves
escaped from Boone and Kenton **counti**es in
Kentucky (about sixteen miles from the Ohio) on
Sunday night last, and **taking** with **the**m two horses
and a sled drove that **night** to **the** Ohio river,
opposite to Western row, in this **city.** Leaving the
horses and sled standing there **they crossed the
river** on foot on **the ice**

DEAD DISNEY MOTHERS

the good queen, mother of snow white: it starts and ends
here – acicular prick in a tall tower, bae bled cradleside

name unknown, mother of a deer: swallowed a sound
like the world's choke, deadheaded on a douchebag's wall

flora, mother of walt: monoxide dream,
·the tiara is a carbon allotrope

igraine, mother of arthur: fucked by magic,
or speared, or an empty grail

name unknown, fox mother: the word *bloodhound*'s
no more a part of the dog than a scream is part of a gun

pocahontas, mother of pocahontas: *amonute, nenamen,*
your whole life between two rivers where I fell and you rose

meredith quill, mother of starlord:
loved a planet of pure light

mrs pelekai, mother of nani and lilo: wet road,
in that last second everything slows down

flora, mother of walt: great mausoleum in
the sanctuary of truth, glendale, los angeles

flora, he couldn't undo it: the gift of summer,
its broken halo, you cannot unwrite fire

MY FATHER AS THE
UNMARKED STATE

Let's say a man falls into a river

No   *someone* falls into a river
A hominid of the homo genus
falls and without
distinguishing details
  cufflinks   side parting   a tendency to do the washing up
   at parties
  you form an image of a person falling
               into a river
Maybe love   maybe love falls into a river   fuck it
A stirring father-of-the-bride speech   sand in the sclera
  bonhomie
  couple of off-colour jokes   falls into a river
All the village elders   all the world's men fall into a river
Luke Perry and Jason Priestley
      fall
Tuesday says *I know we're not halfway yet*
but I've had a week   Tuesday
      falls

 Year 6 falls
My father   white   five foot ten   medium hair
   six children   secure position at IBM
   catalytic converter   falls into a river
Middle C jumps off the great stave
       and falls
The cast of *Friends* falls into a river
My teenage indiscretions

stuff period pants in the outside
bin and fall into a river
The magic of Christmas falls into a river
One of these days   I fucking swear   I'm going to fall into that river
But no   it's my father   falling into a river
Falling still my father
falls into a river
My father   is   was   will be   falling
into a river
We may not reach the other side

IN THE LAST TWO MINUTES OF
ROMAN POLANSKI'S *CHINATOWN*

jack nicholson looks cool and brooding as katherine cross
    is dragged off by the man who raped her mother   nicholson rocks
a classy anthracite fedora   understated threepiece
   and the trademark blend of iconoclasm and
          reluctant moral fibre that has defined him
      as a timeless noir antihero   jj gittes
   played by multi academy award winner nicholson   is all shock
and relatable depth as evelyn mulwray's vitreous humour
       soaks into pleather   joe mantell utters the seminal line
   forget it jake   *it's chinatown*   as katherine goes
to an invisible house   escorted by her father/grandfather
    dress spangled with pieces of faye dunaway   in the last
   two minutes of *chinatown*   rated ninety-nine
      percent on rotten tomatoes   the panavision
   camera stays on jack nicholson's face   in an ending reimagined
by celebrated director roman polanski   from robert towne's original
  script   which saw dunaway escape with her daughter   we close
        on three men in a road   absorbing the tragic
   irony of good intentions   in an ugly world   as somewhere
   katherine lies among bird skeletons   talking to gaps in the brick
    polanski   supported by a who's who of hollywood greats after
sodomising a thirteen-year-old   countered typical silver-
    screen happy endings with this groundbreaking denouement
       which has led many to view *chinatown*
          as one of the greatest films of all time

MARY IS HOLDING JESUS, NOT LIKE A GOD BUT LIKE A BABY, LIKE I WOULD HOLD MY BABY, AND THEY ARE COVERED IN GOLD LIGHT

After David Jones

Mary is blue and turquoise
standing on a hill
geisha cheek and charring
Mary is rain and dusk
planting a bulb with her lips
bare feet in the moss
kindling
Mary is doll white
Mary with a lamb
little love
time still before she'll lose him to the world
the gurning jaws of heaven
spread banquet for the men while she waits outside
but they won't know his yawn like a baby owl
smell of yeast and balm
Mary blue and brimming
the lamb on her lips
a soft moon
crescent of impossible flesh
Mary gold before the trade-off
before he grew infinite
and how she wore it then
stately
metallic

secretly grieving the moon eyes
that would follow her round the room
Mary doesn't remember what sex with God felt like
only the sting of something snapped
Joseph's breath and beard
three men unwrapping
the infant screech of a goat
Mary with thunder that's worse before the coming like a week-
    late period
Mary blue immaculate
blanketed boy on her chest
gone and golden
Mary would listen to all his sermons
scan them for in-jokes
white smoke
a secret message
anything
but this fucking public man
Mary doesn't feel holy
stuffing pigskin in bloody knickers
remembers how she bled for weeks after he came
Mary full of wine
not the warm waters of Galilee
assistant magi
tipsy and trussed up
leotard shine
Mary and thirteen men on her right hand
Mary with a lamb crackling on a spit
when he blessed her
she wanted to spit in his face
tell him *Boy*
I'm the one who wiped away your shit

when the moon came
she sank her teeth in
praying for the sweet-bellied child
she tasted wafer dust
her blue mouth powder stuck
dry as an empty church

MAYBE

It's Saturday and Dad is naked, sitting
in the window of his and Mum's bedroom,
looking out on the front garden, white Astra,
horseshoe viburnum and the crossroad
that brings crash victims to our door
for ambulance calls in a time before mobiles.
Dad – briefcase-swinging father of six – is naked,
arcing in the window, one dangling leg
like a louche question mark and he is singing
– cock, balls and all – to the blue sky. I am
too small to reach the window ledge, big enough
to understand he's not singing because
he is happy. Someone he loves has died,
maybe. Or he's killing the shadow of a life
my mother lived before they met. Decades later,
she will tell me, over pastries, how he drew a door
in the dark years before dying of natural causes.
Dad – bearer of business-trip T-shirts slashed
with Manhattan's broken half smile. There is
so much I don't know. I even made up
the bit about Saturday. I don't know what day
of the week it is when my father, who believes
in God, climbs naked out of a window,
or how many windows he climbed out of
when I wasn't looking, or if people remove
their clothes when they want to remove their skin.
My dad, who was nearly chosen for a role in *Hair*,
has a good voice and when he sings, he can
be heard by all the angels I don't believe in,
and the people on the crossroad. Coat-wearing
strangers who could die at any moment.

i was never more than at fifteen . sick and lovely . see the men
jump out the street to check their shadow . see my high-rise
skirt , glass tights , double-parked eyeliner , apocryphal name ,
smell of monthly embarrassment , suede platforms , scapegoat
thighs , dandruff and blackheads , porn lips , skin lipstick ,
yid nose , cheat bra , cheap heart . men were sick cave-puppies ,
new teeth all over catching sun , rumbling like cars . prepping
the school gates or milling asda , whistle wolves clawing for
cookies they would read my t-shirt . *where you from* and
how old do you think and *how about a* fuckage penetrating
my lopsided ego faith of the worst kind . see the men fall
out the sky to kiss rumour . and my best friend was more .
unequivocally pretty . i would stand next to her and liquify , a
reflect . she get free clothes and steak dinner , pocket money ,
jacuzzi hotel room with businessman . manga face curve child
method actor before the abortion . worshipping her slaves , a
confusion . summer camp eves were a tally of kisses . ugly me
with six but only for telling . i slutted as a macguffin , closing
the narrative of last year : fourteen . see the man with kind face
and chub reading storybooks to me and brother . see his hand
placing under dark the wax and wane of his fingers . see my
atomic . see my roadkill . see my throb tick sunburn aerobic
vomit soft breezing through the house wave like a giant whale
i am in the throat of crest of all downhill best days of your life
enjoy it and stop crying look it's *top of the pops* and kat slater .
i was never more than when i was nothing . i was never i never
did all shhhh and no . i was a pen from melting . objectivity
teething on gobstopper lust i couldn't give away but i gave it .
wet every day like a spaniel's nose . catching flies on the night-
bus , pedalo lake , tube purgatory , blockbusters , park bench ,

trocadero , mcdonald's , bridge belly , cherry tree , corner shop
, rope swing , climbing frame all ironic joy but only wanted or
worthless , i and the rest colouring ourselves in sticky paint
and promise , chewing chat , boys in their t-shirts and genes
bubbling destiny and if love wasn't boy flavour you just kept
quiet love who said anyway who said love no i only . if your
mouth could sing all the animals out of the forest you would ,
wouldn't you . we all method actors pumping puny cocks for
oil waiting for the feelz or feeling daytime soapy drama but
never feeling ourselves . watch out i am so hot i can't even
touch me and days and days of this and not one thing i would
go back for , no not one . did you know if you put enough
posters on your wall you don't need to think , did you know
masturbation is a food group . i am closing on hungry ,
peel my upper lip back , baby , see how you roll right in

HIP, HIP, HOORAH!

FIG.1 (left)   mother. holder of keys.
black ball like a singularity at
their centre. full and fingerless.
sunbeams radiate from her open
mouth and ears the way some
people only exist to music. hear
her. her song is shoulderlift
helicopter, bottlenose front crawl.
bears and ladybirds attend.

FIG.2 (bottom left)   this is a flame raining from the diamond of her crotch. a night she has no door to. it licks the earth like fingers. the taste of soil reminds her of her pregnant body.   its promise.

FIG.3 (centre)   a sheetoverhead ghost.
blue-eyed orange little one sitting on yellow's shoulders. fishtail
down. is it halloween already?

FIG.4 (background)   this is space where a father isn't. cat's cradle of night. you lean into the stretch, turn the night sideways like waking to catch a redeye, pluck comet dust from your nails.

FIG.5 (top right)   this is little old one
eye, his spine beside him, butt
like a hornet metasoma. bulging.
creative. life's work in his liver.
blue heart lugging loose.

FIG.6 (bottom right)   family pup in a
fuzzy numnah. keeper of the
before. black eye punking and full
of prank. sees all, says nothing.

this is the mothersong.
sheetoverhead family. a father she
has no door to. this shoulderlift
only exists to music. bears raining
from the diamond of her redeye.
helicopter down. is it sideways
already? this is space that says
nothing. it turns the night like
fingers. you cradle of liver. you
lean into the music. black eye full
of isn't. this is the

FINDING OUT YOU'RE DEAD BY
WALKING PAST YOUR GRAVE

For J.R.

I ask your name what it's doing on a stone.
It doesn't answer because that's not how names talk.
When I see your name I'm not in a poem and nothing
is the colour of anything else. I'm locked on gravel,
by the loam soil houses of my dad and grandparents
who aren't there, although their names are. Since
your name doesn't have much to say, I ask the stone.
It also doesn't answer. Stone is a dense, unyielding claim
and it is much heavier than a soul, which is why
they put it on top of dead people. When you line stones
up like that, you have a deconstructed guessing game
or a theatre of closed mouths. Your name shines
as if new, as if rain got lost in the shape of someone,
as if nothing, but the dates kill you. I don't know why.
I don't want blame to paint a picture on my phone.
I ask a blank page why it's made of stone and it tells me
a version of a story, and then another. In the versions,
the letters of your name shimmer like sun on the smile
of a razor, shine on curved glass, a puddle in a pothole
or any other thing that takes light from a source
before passing it up to the sky.

RELATIVITY

For my brother, a blank sheet. Start here. Dad of brothers
in orbit, painter of polystyrene planets. Build on, you mother
of worlds. We both had families to become the father
we lost. You do it better than your wayfaring sister.
The sheet will reflect lighter if you lay it in the sun.
Teach me to slow like meltwater, beside a daughter

who also won't. For my sister, the mantle of daughter
whisperer. You grew voices for me and our brother,
SuperTed and Skipper at the table read. If art is the son
of sorrow you gave me colours, said *paint it*. I know our mother
loves you best. It's ok. Even Shakespears Sister
is queen bee when the coast is clear, the view farther.

For my middle sister (wearing the ghost of our father,
mama of cats and kids, never cornflake daughter),
magnetic tape music. Sparked by transistor,
you taught me to sing under ladders. A brother-
hood talisman. I never stopped. You gave me the mother
of all theme tunes. For you, the sun

that stole our brother, whose face rises in your son.
For him, a better beginning, my days with our father
for his years. For my big sister, fairy godmother
of my future, who named me after a beekeeper's daughter
amid fierce flames – green lights, a worthy brother-
in-arms by your side as you bomb through Seven Sisters.

For my mother, as for me, freedom from little sister
syndrome, an eruption of the self, martinis in the sunlight. We are too steeped in the gaze of *big brother*,
still seeking the praise of our long-lost fathers.
For you, the rewilding in your granddaughter's
voice, the hope when I remember that mother

is a verb. For my father, that you forgive our mothers
for not living as cloistered sisters,
see yourself in the unmet eyes of a granddaughter,
see yourself in the furrowed brows of sons.
For you, release from the whalebone cinch of *father* –
crystallised in death's amber. In *Super Mario Bros.*

we ran motherless, sought fathers
in empty castles. Sisters of gold, we were all bros
at circle time, singing *Children of the sun*.

if there is no spark that you are the source

if raptors roam school that your kitchen is infinite

if your dreams never take form that we dance until risen

if we never have money that music

if I die young that your aunties preach against overplucking

if all the days of your life that sometimes

if rain that psalm

if I'm sorry to tell you that elsewhere daybreak

if body is a lie that you are everything imaginable

if minor key footsteps that lightning over easy

if it's wrong that you leave

if love that forgiveness

if you kill someone that I know a place

if the world burns that you build

ZIGGURAT

Hang on a minute while I take the light. There's something here.
This puddle, broken like a wrong egg. On the overpass, rusty
lattice tessellates the magic hour, sighing reservoir. I am younger.
Catch my implicate order as I cross the carriageway, shivering
rainbow-scale skin, slim liquid liner. Look at me here:
no children, no accountant, pain simple, sky a prom dress.
Do you hear that? Shades on, a motorbike. Shades off, lawnmower.
Did you know me then? Squinting at the tiny berries, I whisper –
thank you for keeping me alive and bringing me to this season,
kiss hot vowels at the creaking locks and painted barge names.
Summer's violent music. Come on out from the yellow vetchling.
This is just like you. I remember things that used to work:
the hot crushing of desires into each other, blossom, ring pulls
sweet as rhinestones, cuneiform of wet skin. The world is ours a
little longer. Let's bury it beneath a temple we have yet to build,
on top of which, a smaller temple, on top of which, a smaller
temple, on top of which, the problem with potential is too many
edges, on top of which, I fold in and out, a paper fortune teller in
an eighties playground, on top of which, a smaller temple, on top of
which, a blank score, on top of which, an acorn, damp and ticking.

MU-TH-UR 6000

After Dan O'Bannon

DAY 417

It's impossible to take someone into you without some form of exchange occurring. Not only that, it takes a very long time to take someone into your body; you have to have an enormous amount of patience.

Unable to clarify the extent of the change, the company stated they 'can't allow a carnival that leads to a loss of life in which some human beings don't die but are burnt away'.

DAY 432

The following is a complete list of all the different types of equipment on the ship:

- captive facehuggers in the colony's medical lab
- Arcturian poontang
- Vietnam-era military officer hubris and jargon-veiled incompetence
- the casual arrogance of reeling off a name for nameless terror

DAY 583

All living organisms share a common ancestry. One day, the world's most powerful computer is found in a dusty room. Legend says 'my world will be a living thing. I am still here when night falls.'

Day 1,013

Phylogeny is the study of (1) The family trees of the major groups present in our family, namely, the genera Paramecium, the lineages of the other families, which are divided into those representing terrestrial mammals, birds, reptiles, invertebrates, and fungi; and (2) The branch of the tree of primates, which is divided into those represented in our family (excepting the order Primates), and those represented in the great ape group.

This definition does not include the term 'human' or 'a human being'.

Day 1,014

Every animal is born a xenomorph. In survival case studies, records have confirmed the efficacy of a method known as 'love'.

The speaking clock says 'I'm just glad you're here'.
I'm just glad I'm here.

RECKLESS

Kol ha'olam kulo gesher tzar me'od
—Nachman of Breslav

the thrill of being
skinless, opening
the submarine
window, peeling
a two-minute egg,
forging a pilot
licence. the audacity
of loving someone
this much, of being
allowed to, floodlit
amateur, high
and wild on a rope
that you'll never
stop crossing

FISH BALL SOUP

at Jen Café a man walks in
asking for Mummy
for change I think and half
spin on my bench
check wallet for empty
he's asking for noodle soup
he has five pounds
no you can't get the soup
the owner says
you can get the meal deal
I want the soup I want the pork I want the chicken
this guy
keeps talking
he wants so much while the rest of us sit at our tables shrinking
and quiet
I stare at my condiments
sugar and soy
she makes him a deal but he has to sit outside
he sits and comes back in, Mummy!
sits and comes back
in a film he'd be Jack Sparrow
jangling pheromone festival
here he is dirty grey under fingernails
all loud in our noodles
I know this man
I've fucked him in the treehouse sleeping quarters
of beach bars
met his mama in the village
eaten hot fish with hands

on their floor
but here he is lonely and talks too much
broke and distasteful
here he calls the café owner Mummy
when three people leave
he minesweeps their soup
and I know this man
I have raped his women
I have burned his village
I have taken his clothes
sold them for gold
and baulked at his nakedness
I have plagiarised
and erased him
marched my armies
over every inch of his body
I have crept through his pores
like an ingrowing hair
to attack from inside
I have lied on his faith
whitewashed his walls
spellchecked his tatts
redded his lover's name
he is sitting outside
Mummy takes him a soup
the chicken the pork
he sits and comes back
like there was something
else, still, that he wanted

RULES OF THE QUEST
HOME STORY ARC

The road's ahead of, behind and inside you and there's
nothing more compelling. The side of you that longs
to be swallowed by a higher design craves a twist
in the arc. It's why an ill-advised fuck with an old friend
feels like a return to innocence. Somewhere
on our person we all carry a picture of a garden.

The quest home is a banquet of mini-quests in which
our characters learn vital lessons, acquire surprising skills
like Chamrosh husbandry, and defeat literal demons,
all the while, never losing sight of their goal: a hallowed place
of blurry pictures, moving colours, moans. A woman,
a sunbeam, a yearbook. At the moment of truth,

cut to the credits. Not to the next bit: waking after an
eighteen-hour syncope in a bed smaller than remembered,
coffee with the longed-for friend who walks you through
their bathroom remodel in meticulous detail, the night
at the window, air-full, pleading with the star you followed,
There's been a mistake. Show me again, please, show me again.

ALI TALKS ME THROUGH
THE MULTIVERSE

I've been trying to tell this story for a long time. I remember holding my infant father in my arms. Only the faintest note, but once you've heard the clang-snap of an assault rifle being gathered you'll know it on every street you walk. Our bodies are at war with us forever and all I got was this lousy T-shirt. I couldn't save him. I'm forever walking into rooms as if I'm walking out of them. My sister leaves a room and suddenly, the corridor is the place to be. Her brain used to take her away, sometimes just a few seconds, mid-castling, a falling tonic of chess pieces and I always wondered where she went, if it was like Laura Palmer in the Black Lodge. There is a universe where you ate Coco Pops instead of Shreddies. Pinot on Zoom. There is a universe where you wore boots and, lacing, missed your train. Before we were mothers, we were people: drunk on the carpet in devil horns, lying to the chorus. There is a universe where you caught the train and it was hit by a crashing Dornier. Endless forks; things that seem mutually exclusive can coexist for years without anyone noticing. There is a universe where you exploded, blood hitting the air like stars. At primary, Mr Eccles was everyone's favourite teacher: warm and kind and, of course, he died young. The school gave a weekly award in his name. Years later, stories came out. Strange touching during PE. A live fish in your hand, dead fox on the school run. What do we do with that? When I look for my father, he is standing behind the glass of a new-build office that looks out on a city side street. It's Bring Your Kids to Work Day and we're typing notes to each other on Acorn computers, alien green on federal black. I try to pick him out through the floor-to-ceiling windows but the glass is flushed with sunlight. I don't know which one of us is inside.

ON ROLLING A JOINT
FOR YOUR MOTHER,

you will channel a deftness that eludes you, some sleight
of eye that hones you to hold you better. Forget
the rolling mat that saw you through fresherhood,
the saggy sleeping bags smoked in the 6 a.m. recourse of a
dreaming room, the wrong-sided skins left you
licking a nameless state. You're not playing now.
You came all this way. Today, you are bending
to a dresser as if you were kneeling at the door
of a tree, while thinking how we arrive in pain,
how pain is a warning that yes, you are alive, and still
you will tell the tree that this woman, phone full
of children eating, this woman typing in the dark,
this woman, who held you like night holds colour
in a night that began you, is alive enough. You will
kneel unskilled before the tree, hold its face until paper
unpeels from bark and lies down, and your faith
will scatter, but not crumble, on the upturned prism
of these pages on which are written your entire life.

HACKNEY ROAD

for David Gould

you step lightly into the room
halfway through my blow dry,
lean against the sideboard
while he straightens my ends.
you are there, chilling
as he rounds off the corners.
it's a relief, your arrival.
I have been waiting for it
like I wait every year
for time to drop me back
into the current, for the break
of cloud and fever
that feels like being held.
he spins me round to the small
mirror. you are there,
calm like you have all the
world's time, because you do.
and quiet, you follow me home,
stay until morning,
sun strobe heat and haptic,
until the hour comes
and you turn, again

T-MINUS ZERO

it won't matter if the water
   is hot or cold
it won't matter about the plastic
   tub for the placenta
or which pyjamas
when you lie on a floor
   next to the lift
trolleys
splash rocky down corridors
   each

contraction a red
   sun setting over and
in you

rise out of water
   his eyes catching you
falling into the room
   when she swells
into the water

a tree
   splitting to give way
to lightning

her head like god
   cracking
a rock a planet a red sun
   rising blood
won't matter

frog slither neck
   and shoulders
and he in the sun all kneeling
your hands full of someone
slick minute
   god

when she comes
   you won't remember if she cried
because
look
look at the day
arriving
   someone is here

Notes

'In the Wet-Aired Trenches of the Tube I Was' is about postnatal anxiety, thought to affect up to thirty per cent of new mothers.

'Billie, Blinded by Grace' borrows the titular phrase from Stormzy's 'Blinded by Your Grace Pt.2' which appears on the album *Gang Signs & Prayer*. The lines 'There is a witch, a ginger plait, dog, / bird, frog, dragon' are a reference to Julia Donaldson's *Room on the Broom*.

'Atheism' is inspired by pelvic organ prolapse, thought to affect up to fifty per cent of AFAB people, although studies vary between 3-68% prevalence, possibly because of the number of people who don't report their symptoms or seek medical advice, due to shame and a lack of information.

'The Year of the Horse' uses words and phrases first recorded in print in 1990, according to the Merriam-Webster Time Traveler tool.

'See Also' is composed largely of found text from websites including Wikidiff.com and Wikipedia.

'Dance on My Grave' takes its title from the Aidan Chambers YA novel of the same name, published in 1982: one of the first YA books to feature a gay-positive storyline.

'Ice Baby' is written in response to the Mississippi ICE raids in August 2019, in which over 680 undocumented workers were arrested at food processing plants across six cities.

'Margaret Garner Will Have Her Revenge on Kentucky' is comprised entirely of text from the article 'Arrest of Fugitive Slaves. A Slave Mother Murders her Child rather than see it Returned to Slavery.' which appeared in the *Cincinnati Gazette*, January 29, 1856, and is available in the Cincinnati History Library and Archives, Cincinnati Museum Center.

'Dead Disney Mothers' references the death of Walt Disney's mother Flora Call Disney, a result of a furnace leak in the North Hollywood house Walt and Roy Disney bought for their parents.

'My Father as the Unmarked State' is informed by Chapter 3: The Unmarked State in *Writing the Other* by Nisi Shawl and Cynthia Ward.

'Mary Is Holding Jesus, Not Like a God but Like a Baby, Like I Would Hold My Baby, and They Are Covered in Gold Light' is written after the painting 'Madonna and Child in a Landscape' by David Jones.

'every girl knows' uses syntax inspired by Eimear McBride's novel *A Girl Is a Half-Formed Thing*.

'Hip, Hip, Hoorah!' is written as an accompaniment to the Karel Appel painting of the same name.

'Relativity' references the lyric 'I'm a queen bee when the coast is clear' from the 1989 single 'You're History' by Shakespears Sister.

'MU-TH-UR 6000' is the Nostromo's ship computer in the film *Alien* (also known informally as 'MOTHER'). The poem includes found text from the arstechnica.com article 'The throwaway line in *Aliens* that spawned decades of confusion' and the Talk to Transformer neural network.

Acknowledgements

Thanks are due to the editors of *Aesthetica, the Adriatic, Ambit, bath magg, Culture Matters, fourteen poems, PERVERSE, PN Review, The Poetry Review, the Rialto, the Scores, Spontaneous Poetics, Tears in the Fence, Tentacular, Verve Poetry Press* and *The White Review*, who first published versions of some of these poems.

'every girl knows' won the Verve Poetry Competition. 'In the Last Two Minutes of Roman Polanski's Chinatown' was shortlisted for the Aesthetica Creative Writing Award. 'Billie, Blinded by Grace' was commended in the Winchester Poetry Prize. Several poems appeared in the pamphlet *And They Are Covered in Gold Light* (Bad Betty Press, 2019).

Profound thanks to my editor Kayo Chingonyi, who helped me to see the world within the work more clearly. Thanks also to Martha Sprackland for astute and generous copyediting, to Greg Heinimann for the beautiful cover, to Laura Jones and to all at Bloomsbury.

Endless gratitude to Liz Berry, the midwife of this collection, whose early belief in the book gave me courage.

Many poets and friends have contributed to this book's development through feedback, support and solidarity, including Clare Pollard, Matthew Caley, Joelle Taylor, Salena Godden, Sasha Dugdale, Mark Waldron, Jo Davis, Nicki Heinen, Anne Macaulay, Anja Konig, Jonathan Catherall, Naomi Woddis and Ali Cunningham. Thank you all.

Countless friends and supporters have contributed to my development as a poet, whether by collaborating, advising, endorsing or giving my work a platform. Thank you Niall O'Sullivan, Roddy Lumsden, Degna Stone, A. B. Jackson, Luke Kennard, Denise Saul, Colette Brice, Fran Lock, Rebecca Tamás, Katie Bonna, Richard Marsh, Peter Hayhoe, Anna Le, Jamie Cameron, Sam Bourke, and Max Lowe.

Thank you to the Poetry School, the Arvon Foundation, flipped eye publishing, the Poetry Book Society and Arts Council England.

Thanks and love to all my Bad Betty Press family.

Love to my extended poetry family, my friends, and especially to my family: Gillian, David, Aaron, Rachel, Livy, Natalie and Brian. To Billie and Solomon. To my Hall family.

This book is dedicated to my daughter, but it also belongs to Jake Wild Hall – my husband, co-parent, co-publisher and best friend: whose

energy, insight, support, love, laughs and kind-
ness have been the making of me.

A Note on the Author

Amy Acre is a poet and writer, and the editor of Bad Betty Press. Her pamphlets *And They Are Covered in Gold Light* (Bad Betty, 2019) and *Where We're Going, We Don't Need Roads* (flipped eye, 2015) were each chosen as a Poetry Book Society Pamphlet Choice. Her work has been selected as a BBC Pick of the Week, and published in the *Poetry Review*, *Poetry London*, *The White Review* and elsewhere. Her poem 'every girl knows' won the 2019 Verve Poetry Prize. She's written for BBC Radio 4 and featured on the Last Dinosaur's 2020 track, 'In The Belly of a Whale'. Amy was born and raised in London, and lives in Nottingham. *Mothersong* is her first collection.

A Note on the Type

Warnock is a serif typeface designed by Robert Slimbach. The design features sharp, wedge-shaped serifs. The typeface is named after John Warnock, one of the co-founders of Adobe. John Warnock's son, Chris Warnock, requested that Slimbach design the typeface as a tribute to his father in 1997. It was later released as a commercial font by Adobe in 2000 under the name Warnock Pro.

MORE FROM BLOOMSBURY POETRY

If you enjoyed *Mothersong*, you might like

Sonnets for Albert by Anthony Joseph:

Fire for you, and the mothers of the church lit candles
upon your breastbone. Fire was lit, even in the hole
to purify the earth to receive you. They poured flame
from brass goblets of croton and pink ixora.
And swung a chant to kill death:
                    O Death, draw out your sword.